Are You Smarter Than a SHARK?

Written by
David George Gordon
Illustrated by
Josh Lynch

Published in 2021 by becker&mayer! kids, an imprint of The Quarto Group,
11120 NE 33rd Place, Suite 201, Bellevue, WA 98004 USA.
www.QuartoKnows.com

---

becker&mayer! kids titles are also available at discount for retail, wholesale, promotional, and bulk purchase. For details, contact the Special Sales Manager by email at specialsales@quarto.com or by mail at The Quarto Group, Attn: Special Sales Manager, 100 Cummings Center Suite 265D, Beverly, MA 01915 USA.

21 22 23 24 25   5 4 3 2 1

ISBN: 978-0-7603-7296-8

Digital edition published in 2021
eISBN: 978-0-7603-7046-9

Library of Congress Cataloging-in-Publication Data available upon request.

Author: David George Gordon
Illustration: Josh Lynch

Printed, manufactured, and assembled in Huizhou, China, 04/21.

FSC www.fsc.org MIX Paper from responsible sources FSC® C016973

Image credits: Design elements © Shutterstock.com

#346499

Contents

Child's play!

Shark Smarts

Sharks don't write books or build rocket ships, but that doesn't mean they aren't smart.

Sharks have their own way of thinking. This way of thinking makes them one of the top *predators* in the ocean. A mouth full of razor-sharp teeth helps, too.

Like humans, sharks use their senses of sight, hearing, taste, touch, and smell. These senses help them pick up clues from the world around them. Sharks also have a special "sixth sense" to help them survive.

Shark Basics

Sharks are fish that live in the ocean. There are more than 400 kinds of sharks. Some kinds of sharks are dangerous to people. Most would rather stay as far away from us as possible.

No Bone Zone

Most fish have bones inside their bodies. Sharks don't have bones. Instead, their skeletons are made of cartilage (CART-eh-ledge). That's the bendy stuff that gives support to your ears and nose.

Sharks Around the World

Sharks swim in all the world's oceans. A few kinds even make their homes in rivers and lakes. Greenland sharks prowl the icy waters of the North Pacific and Arctic oceans. Nurse sharks rest on the sandy bottom of shallow reefs in the Atlantic and Pacific oceans. Thresher sharks are found in all the world's temperate oceans. You can find sharks all over the world!

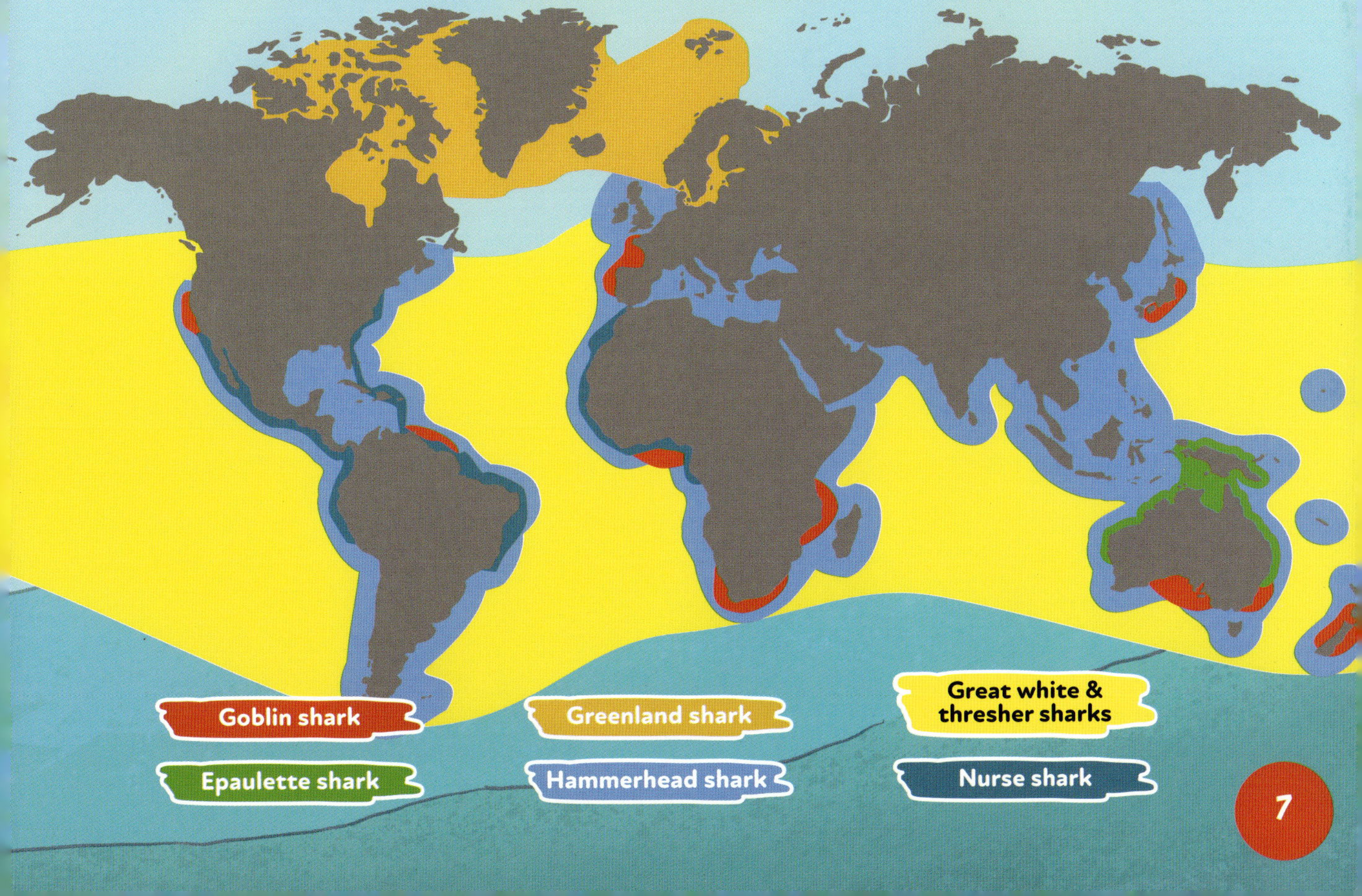

Shark Anatomy

The sleek, muscular body of a shark is designed for gliding through the water. Zigzag bands of muscle move the rear half of the body from side to side. Each flat, stiff fin serves a special purpose.

GREAT WHITE AND MAKO SHARKS USE THEIR POWERFUL MUSCLES TO LEAP OUT OF THE WATER. THIS IS CALLED BREACHING.

Brainwaves

Much of your brain is used to think, plan, imagine, learn, and remember. Compared to your brain, a shark's brain is small and simple. Shark brains tell them where to find food—and how not to become food for others. A great white shark's brain is made up of three main parts:

The **forebrain** takes in signals about smells in the water. A few drops of blood from an injured fish let the shark know that dinner will soon be served.

Areas in the **midbrain** are connected to the shark's eyes.

The **hindbrain** is in charge of the shark's swimming motions. It also helps the shark's balance. If its hindbrain is damaged, a shark will stop swimming.

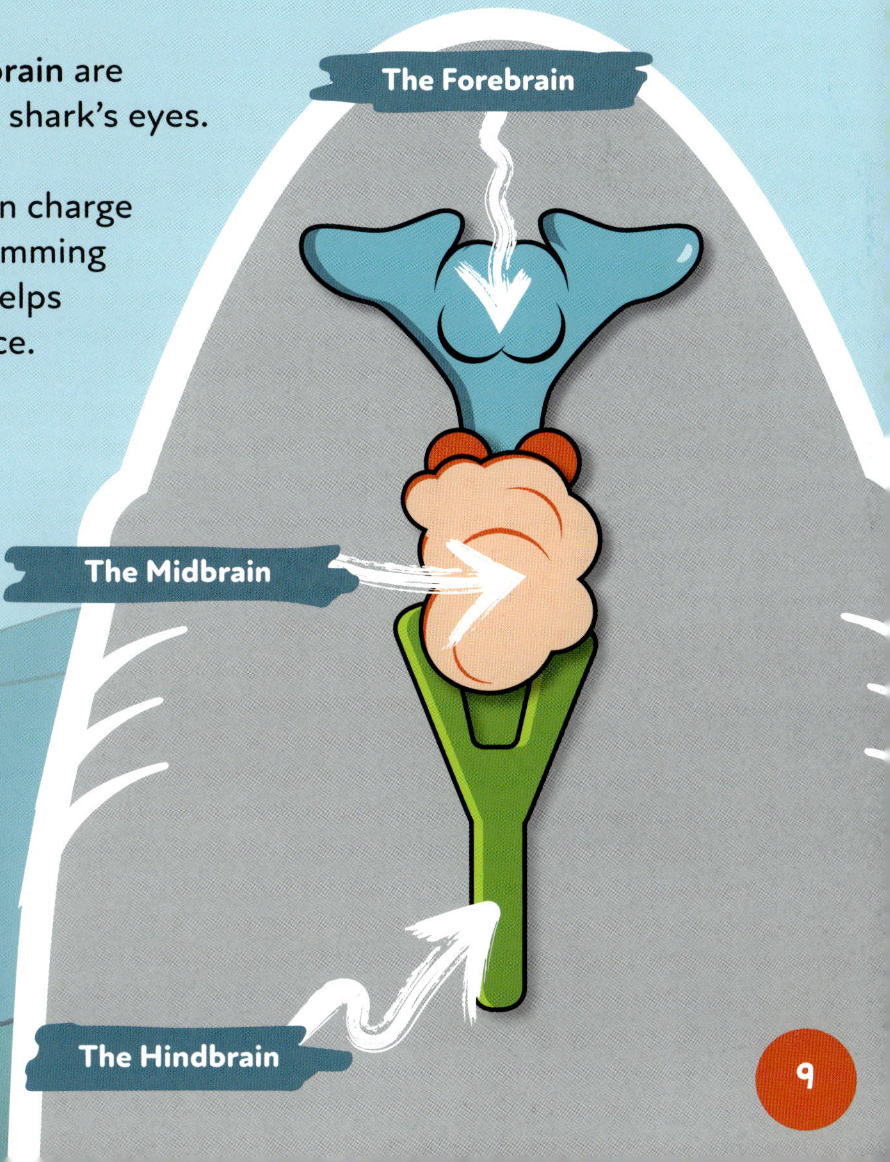

Megalodon

THE NAME MEGALODON MEANS "BIG TEETH."

In the Beginning

Sharks were swimming in the oceans long before the first dinosaurs walked on land. The oldest known shark was Elegestolepis (el-uh-JEST-oh-lep-eez). It lived more than 400 million years ago. No one knows what it looked like.

Some prehistoric sharks were bigger than a school bus. The biggest and baddest was Megalodon (MEG-uh-luh-dawn). Megalodon opened its jaws about eight feet!

Unlike its giant cousin Megalodon, the prehistoric shark falcatus (fal-KAY-tus) was only about as long as a pencil.

The early shark Stethancanthus (STEH-than-CAN-thuss) had a dorsal fin that looked like an ironing board.

THE NAME "SHARK" WAS FIRST USED BY BRITISH SAILORS IN THE LATE 1600S. THEY MAY HAVE LEARNED THIS WORD FROM NATIVES OF SOUTH AMERICA. SOON OTHERS STARTED USING IT, AND THE NAME STUCK.

What Makes Sharks Smart?

Sharks, and other animals, can't answer our questions with words. To see if sharks are smart, scientists look at several things. Here are four.

1. **Can sharks learn?** Yes! Sharks can be taught to recognize shapes and colors. Some clever sharks can tell the difference between the front and back of a person. This lets them make sneak attacks from behind.

2. **Can sharks remember what they have learned?** Yes! Some sharks have very good memories. In tests, sharks have been taught that a certain sound means "food is on the way." Months later, when they hear the same sound, the sharks will wait for their food to show up.

3. **Are sharks curious?** Yes! When something new is put into its tank, a shark will bump the object with its nose. What happens next will tell the shark if the object is dangerous or friendly—or even good to eat. The curious shark wants to find out right away. That's smart.

4 **Are sharks playful?** Yes! Sharks will play with objects they find floating in the sea. There's no real purpose to such play. It's just fun. Only the brainiest animals play. Nature's best players include octopuses, ravens, seals, monkeys, dolphins, and people.

It All Makes Sense!

Sharks use their senses to understand the world around them. The shark's eyes, ears, nose, and other senses send signals to the brain through a system of nerves. These nerves are spread throughout the body. They look like the branches of a tree. The trunk of this tree is called the spinal cord. The spinal cord sends the signals to the brain.

UNLIKE HUMANS, MOST SHARKS ARE COLD-BLOODED. THAT MEANS THEIR BODY TEMPERATURE IS THE SAME AS THE WATER AROUND THEM.

Sense Tests

Humans have five major senses, just like sharks. These senses are sight, sound, smell, taste, and touch. Sharks have those five senses in common with us! In the next part of the book, you will get a chance to test yours senses against a shark's.

I wonder how fresh those tires are?
I don't know, but this all looks good to me!
Nom nom!

What's for Dinner?

Sharks are not picky eaters. They are predators. Predators are animals that hunt other animals for food. Their favorite live foods include seals, sea lions, fish, crabs, lobsters, and seabirds. But they'll eat just about anything, including trash.

Horn sharks and other slow-goers search for clams, oysters, and other sea life buried in the sandy seafloor. Active feeders, like dogfish, hunt in packs of several hundred. They search together for big schools of fish or squid. Great white sharks are fast-swimming loners. They chase after seals and sea lions all by themselves.

A few sharks have been known to eat people. That's probably because, when viewed from below, people look a lot like their favorite food, seals. A shark might take a bite of a person before quickly spitting it out.

The Taste Test

Is your sense of taste better than a shark's? Try this test with a friend.

For this experiment, one of you will be the taste-tester and the other will be the test-runner. You'll need a blindfold, paper and pencil, and five lollipops of different colors and flavors. Examples are orange (orange), root beer (brown), lemon-lime (green), cherry (red), and grape (purple).

1. On a sheet of paper, write down the five flavors. Give each a number, one to five.
2. The taste-tester puts on the blindfold and then licks each lollipop, one at a time. After one lick only, the taste-tester says what flavor the lollipop is.
3. The test-runner writes down the answers.
4. After all five lollipops are licked, read the answers aloud. How often was the taste-tester right?

Because our sense of taste is not always the best, we may need to see the lollipop's color to get the flavor right. Even so, your sense of taste is much better than a shark's.

Food or Not Food

Sharks have tastebuds all over the inside of the mouth and throat. Scientists think that taste buds and teeth may have come from the same kinds of cells, millions of years ago. However, it appears that sharks cannot tell the difference between sweet, sour, salty, and bitter. To a shark, a full stomach is more important than a delicious meal.

A Toothy Tool Kit

A shark's teeth are made of calcium, just like yours. Behind the shark's first row of teeth is another row waiting to take its place. Some sharks have 15 rows of teeth!

Sharks' teeth lack roots to keep them firmly in place. Sharks lose and replace teeth throughout their lives. They may lose more than 20,000 teeth over their lifetime.

NOT ALL SHARKS HAVE TEETH. WATER FLOWS THROUGH THE GILLS OF BASKING SHARKS AND WHALE SHARKS, WHICH STRAIN OUT TINY SHRIMP-LIKE PLANKTON CALLED KRILL.

Basking shark

Feeding Frenzy

When there is plenty of food around, the sharks may start a feeding frenzy. That's a gathering of hungry sharks that will snap at just about anything, dead or alive. Fishermen have found tin cans, rubber tires, lobster traps, and even a suit of armor inside shark stomachs.

The Tooth Test

Can you tell the difference between shark teeth? Try this test in your kitchen.

You have different kinds of teeth in your mouth. Take a bite of food. Which teeth do you use for biting? Which ones do you use for chewing? For other types of jobs, you probably need some tools.

Ask a grownup to give you a tour of your kitchen's utensil drawer. See if they can show you a steak knife, a carving fork, a can opener, and a nutcracker. Would a shark need any of these items? Definitely not.

Can opener

A tiger shark's teeth are rounded. One surface is smooth and another is jagged. This is just the ticket for cutting through super-hard materials without chipping or breaking.

Carving fork

A goblin shark sticks its long, slender teeth into squid to hold it in place.

Steak knife

The jagged edges of great white shark teeth saw pieces of meat from the bone. The shark swallows the chunks whole—no chewing required.

Nutcracker

Row upon row of big, flat teeth inside the gummy shark's mouth are great for crushing the hard shells of crabs and other seafloor creatures. This lets the shark eat the tender meat inside.

Getting Nosy

A shark's nose doesn't look anything like yours. On the underside of the shark's snout, you will see two small holes right in front of its mouth. Those are the shark's nostrils. A shark uses its nostrils for smelling only, not for breathing.

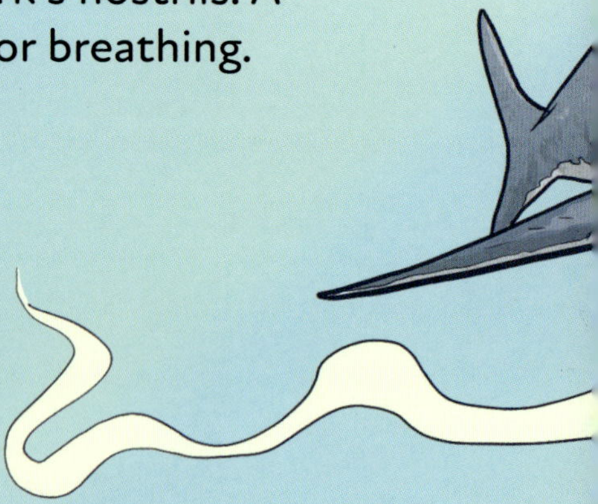

What a Shark Nose

A shark's sense of smell is much better than yours. The nostrils detect teeny scent particles in the water.

As it swims, a shark slowly sweeps its head and body from side-to-side. If a scent reaches one nostril first, the shark will turn in that direction in search of food.

Is that pineapple on that pizza?
Pineapple? I LOVE pineapple!
No, you don't. You're a shark.

The Sniff Test

Can you smell like a shark? Try this delicious test the next time your family orders pizza.

1. Ask your family to add an extra secret—but a little bit smelly—ingredient, such as onions, sausage, or anchovies. Ask them to not tell you what they ordered.

2. When the pizza arrives—but before opening the box—take a moment to breathe in and out through your nose. Now make a guess—can you "smell out" what the extra topping is?

3. Open the box. Were you right?

Sharks don't use their noses for breathing. They breathe with gills, which take in oxygen from the water.

Do you think my new glasses make me look smart?
Not when you wear them like that!

Deep "Sees"

Sharks have good vision, about the same as ours. However, they don't use their eyesight that much. Floating bits of plankton, algae, and dirt limit how far a shark can see. At night, when the sun sets over the ocean, there are no streetlights to show sharks the way.

Seeing from Eye to Eye

Hammerhead sharks have widely spaced eyes on the ends of their hammer-shaped heads. Hammerheads might look scary, but they rarely attack people. There is even a kind of hammerhead, called the bonnethead shark, that nibbles on seagrasses. It's like a little lamb of the sea.

BECAUSE MOST SHARKS HAVE TO KEEP MOVING TO KEEP BREATHING, THEY DO NOT SLEEP IN THE SAME WAY THAT HUMANS DO.

The Vision Test

Can you see like a shark? Try to find someone without using your eyes. You'll need a friend or adult assistant for this test.

1. On a playground or other safe, open area, close your eyes.
2. Ask your assistant to stand next to you and start talking in a normal voice.
3. Ask them to move around you in a circle while still talking. Can you point to where they are just by hearing the direction of their voice?
4. Now ask them to stop talking, move farther away from you, and then change where they are standing.
5. When they start talking again, can you still point to where they are standing?

Instead of using their eyes to lead them to food, sharks use their other senses—mostly hearing and smell.

Watery Sound Waves

Sharks don't have big ears—just little holes on the sides of their heads. But even with those tiny ears, sharks can hear the splashing of an injured fish nearly a football field's distance away.

Good Vibrations

Sound is a wave that is created by vibrations. Particles pass the vibrations to the particles next to them. Water is more packed with particles than air, so sound moves faster through water. This makes it easier for sharks to hear things while they are cruising along.

SHARKS HAVE SPECIAL NERVES THAT RECOGNIZE VIBRATIONS THROUGH THE WATER, SUCH AS FISH. THIS IS CALLED THE "DISTANT TOUCH" SYSTEM.
I don't know how I hear ANYTHING with these tiny ear-holes.
Yeah, but can you imagine how silly I would look with human ears sticking out to the sides?
At least I wouldn't keep losing my earrings!

The Tap Test

1. Fill your bathtub with warm water and gently lower yourself in. Sit up, keeping your head, shoulders, and one hand above the waterline.

2. Using the fingers of the dry hand, give the rim of the tub a gentle tap. Would you say that the tap was very loud?

3. Now lower your head and shoulders so that your ears are under water. With the same hand as before, give the tub another tap. Did this second tap sound louder? That's because sound travels better in water than it does in the air.

Little Shark, Big Danger

Sharks use their hearing to stay safe from storms, forgotten fishing nets, orca whales and even other sharks. Some sharks, which hatch from eggs known as mermaid's purses, can detect evidence of these dangers from inside the eggs. When the time is right, the egg case splits open. The baby shark swims out!

Do you like my fancy skin pattern?
To be honest, I barely noticed you.
All this talk is making my skin crawl.
Blue shark
Spotted Wobbegong
Izak cat shark

Skin Teeth

Shark don't have smooth scales like other fish. Instead, their skin is bumpy. It's covered with tiny "skin-teeth" called *dermal denticles*. The bumps make the skin scratchy to the touch.

Years ago, people sanded the wooden masts of ships with shark skin instead of sandpaper. In Japan, some sword handles were wrapped in shark skin. The rough surface made the swords easier to grip.

Hide and Seek

Many sharks have dark backs and pale bellies. This pattern is called *countershading*. It's a great way to blend in. Looking up at a shark from below, the pale belly blends in with the light-colored surface of the water. Looking down from above, the dark back matches the ocean water below.

CARPET SHARKS, SUCH AS THE SPOTTED WOBBEGONG, ARE COVERED WITH BOLD SWIRLS OF COLOR THAT MATCH THE CORAL ON TROPICAL REEFS.

Extra Sensory

Sharks have an extra sense that you don't have. This sense lets them feel the electrical currents that all living things produce. These currents are what make your heart beat, your muscles move, and your brain think.

It's the Pits

Small dots on a shark's snout and head called *ampullae of Lorenzini* pick up electrical signals. The signals give the shark a picture of anything that is buried in the sand or hiding nearby. It's like having a built-in metal detector or a super-power!

Beware These Bites

Lots of people think sharks attacks are common. But fewer than three dozen kinds of sharks are dangerous to people. Here are four types of sharks that can cause harm.

DANGER

GREAT WHITE SHARK

RECORDED ATTACKS: MORE THAN 300
LENGTH: 13–21 FEET (4-6.5 METERS)
WEIGHT: 5,000 POUNDS (2300 KILOGRAMS)
TOP SPEED: 15 MPH (24 KPH)

Great whites are the largest predatory fish in the sea.

DANGER

TIGER SHARK

RECORDED ATTACKS: MORE THAN 100
LENGTH: 10–14 FEET (3.5-4.5 METERS)
WEIGHT: 850–1,400 POUNDS (385-635 KILOGRAMS)
TOP SPEED: 20 MPH (32 KPH)

Tiger sharks hunt mostly at night. People call them "garbage cans with fins."

DANGER

SHORTFIN MAKO

RECORDED ATTACKS: UNKNOWN
LENGTH: 10.5–12.5 FEET (3.5-4 METERS)
WEIGHT: UP TO 1,250 POUNDS (UP TO 570 KILOGRAMS)
TOP SPEED: 50 MPH (80 KPH)

This superfast swimmer can leap 20 feet out of the water!

DANGER

BULL SHARK

RECORDED ATTACKS: 69
LENGTH: UP TO 11.5 FEET (UP TO 4 METERS)
WEIGHT: UP TO 500 POUNDS (UP TO 225 KILOGRAMS)
TOP SPEED: 25 MPH (40 KPH)

Bull sharks enter tropical river systems, where people are most likely to swim.

Winghead shark
Brier shark
Cookie cutter shark
Whale shark
Frilled shark
Spotted Wobbegong

One Big, Toothy Family

Let's face it, I have the strangest cousins.

Finny Friends

Rays, skates, sawfish, guitarfish, and ratfish are all relatives of sharks. Like sharks, their skeletons are made of cartilage.

The **manta ray** is the largest member of the ray family, which includes the stingray. Their smaller cousin, the **electric ray,** stuns its prey with electric currents.

Sawfish have special electric senses to get around in the dark, muddy waters they like to swim in.

The ratfish sports a long pointed tail and *venomous* spine on its back.

Whoever first named the **guitarfish** thought it looked like a musical instrument without strings. But who wants to play this flat bottom-dweller? The guitarfish has a row of sharp spines on its back. It has spikes over its eyes, too.

Stingrays spend most of their time resting on the ocean floor. Small holes behind their eyes let them breathe, even while buried in the sand. The **blue spotted stingray** has two sharp, venomous spines at the base of its tail.

STOP
OVERFISHING
SAVE THE
SHARKS
WE NEED
YOUR HELP

Save the Sharks

Even though humans are dangerous to sharks, they can also be helpful. Here are some ways you can help save what is left of these amazing animals.

Follow the Law

It is against the law to kill great white sharks, whale sharks, and many other kinds. Still, some people hunt them for shark meat, fins, and jaws. Several kinds of sharks are now endangered and might one day become extinct.

Don't Take Too Much

Overfishing happens when people catch too many fish for food. When that happens, sharks have trouble finding the food they need.

Protect Their Habitats

Nurseries are places where baby sharks can hide, find food, and grow into adults. We humans need to protect these safe places. Without sharks in our oceans, the balance of nature would be different.

Here are some organizations that work to keep sharks safe:

- NOAA Fisheries
- Wildlife Conservation Society
- World Wildlife Fund
- Coral Reef Alliance
- Shark Stewards

Glossary of Shark Terms

Ampullae of Lorenzini: Sensory organs that detect electric fields.

Barbel: A small spine or bristle that grows from the mouth, snout, or chin of a fish.

Breaching: Leaping above the water's surface.

Countershading: An animal's way of blending in with its surroundings; parts normally viewed from below are light and those viewed from above are dark.

Dermal denticles: Small scales on a shark's skin that look like tiny teeth.

Extinct: No living members exist.

Fin: A wing-like body part attached to the body of a fish.

Gill: An organ that allows fish to breathe oxygen from the water.

Intelligence: The ability to learn and understand.

Lateral line: A row of sense organs along the side of a fish; used for detecting pressure and vibration.

Nurseries: A sheltered area where young sharks can grow and mature.

Plankton: Groups of small drifting plants and animals that float in the sea.

Predators: Animals that hunt or prey on other animals for food.

Ray: A type of fish with a flattened body, broad fins, gill slits on the underside, and eyes on the top of its head.

Temperate: Waters where the temperature is around 50 degrees.

Venomous: Able to inject a substance that can harm or kill a living thing.